"This book is dedicated to my grandfather, my baba who has always been my inspiration and hero!"

I hope this makes you proud baba!

STRAIGHT FROM MY HEART

Volume -2

KAHAAN KHAITAN

ZORBA BOOKS

Published by Zorba Books, August 2022
Website: www.zorbabooks.com
Email: info@zorbabooks.com

Author Name & Copyright © Kahaan Khaitan

Title:- Straight From My Heart, Volume -2

Printbook ISBN :- 978-93-93029-92-8
Ebook ISBN :- 978-93-93029-93-5

Zorba Books Pvt. Ltd. (opc)
Sushant Arcade,
Next to Courtyard Marriot,
Sushant Lok 1, Gurgaon – 122009, India

Printed by Thomson Press (India) Ltd.
B-315, Okhla Industrial Area, Phase 1, New Delhi- 110020

Contents

About The Author

Kahaan Khaitan hails from New Delhi- the capital of India. He finished his schooling from the prestigious St. Columba's School (Delhi) and graduated with a Bachelors degree in Business Administration from Babson College, Boston. His passion for writing poetry developed after moving back to India and his inspiration stems from his own relationships and the plethora of emotions we go through in every- day life. Kahaan has penned two poetry books by the names Straight from my Heart and Ignite the spark which was co authored by his wife Vedika Khaitan. This is his third work. Presently he is working in his family business and along with writing poems, He has started House of Hope along with his friend Nikita Gupta. House of Hope is a humanitarian project that helps to develop and nurture underprivileged children. With house of Hope he focuses on spreading smiles and hope in the society by undertaking projects like lighting villages, giving warm clothes to the needy in the winters or adopting government schools wherein he distributes smart phones.

Kahaan is a passionate individual who wants to keep writing on varied topics and growing in life with his experiences.

# Foreward

More so than most, Kahaan thinks of others. More rare, however, is that he goes beyond merely thinking, and does.

This quality shines through always – be it buying an ice-cream for an 'Ice-cream Wallah' (a pejorative term, as in India and certainly Delhi we would rather just call the gent bhaiyya or uncle), treating street kids (another questionable term, one that masks these children's daily struggles) to warm clothes and a meal, or quite literally bringing light to the lives of hundreds, as he has done now several times with his lovely wife Vedika through their organization House of Hope.

Kahaan routinely lifts people, from being a term or a stranger, always seeing the humanity within. It is so rare a trait, and one he himself is too modest to state. Kahaan is also a fierce friend. Be it driving hundreds of kilometres just for a meal, promoting a friends' business without a second thought, or even making unrepeatable jokes on a whatsapp group (the group shall go unnamed), he is the sort of friend you read about. Let alone be lucky enough to have in your life.

So when I was asked to pen a foreword for Kahaan's latest book, I knew that the words would not be difficult to find.

When I think of Kahaan, three words come immediately to mind: generous, innocent, prolific. Generosity is at the very core of Kahaan. His innocence has remained unchanged since I first met him as a freshie in undergrad or when I talk to the man who is now a father. He is also prolific – balancing work, family, social/ community service work, his love of poetry, and no doubt other responsibilities all while maintaining his unique band of humour.

All three words and qualities come to the fore in this book, in what is now his third poetry anthology. It paints also a picture of growth, vulnerability, passage of time, and ultimately, abundance. Of life and of character.

Something Kahaan possesses in spades.

Ashwin Bhat

Singapore

Foreward

Nearly ten years ago, while working on a farm in Costa Rica, I remembered the beauty of letting go. At the time, I'd felt physically and spiritually called to Costa Rica — a place where I could connect to all the natural elements — the forests, oceans and rivers, volcanoes, and fresh air. All of this could be summarized by the local phrase "pura vida," which translates to a pure or simple life.

Before traveling to Costa Rica, I had most looked forward to seeing the blue morpho butterfly — a bright, luminescent creature that I'd been visualizing for over a year. After several weeks, I had missed every encounter. Friends on the farm would notice the butterflies, but I would turn around just in time to watch them disappear.

One Saturday morning, I woke up feeling a deep, joyful peace. I walked out of the communal cabin, and headed over to the spring~water pool, where the sun shined brightest. I closed my eyes and took a deep breath, smiling as I felt the warm sun rays kiss my eyelids. In that moment, I felt a profound reminder that I was a part of everything in the universe, and everything was a part of me.

When I opened my eyes, just a couple feet from my face was a blue morpho butterfly fluttering around the pool. I was so excited. Excited to experience what felt like an intimate moment with the universe. Excited to have manifested this butterfly's presence. Excited to finally witness its beauty close~up.

But that moment of divine joy was also sprinkled with my ego. I screamed when I saw what I had manifested. And in what seemed like a split second, the blue morpho butterfly was gone.

Energetically, I had shifted from being present, open, and connected to being distracted, fearful, and possessive. I chased after the butterfly, but it was too late.

I started laughing at the irony. When I trusted my connection to everything around me, and stopped "wanting," I attracted everything I'd wanted. But the moment I tried to hold onto what I'd received, I lost it.

Straight From the Heart: Volume 2 reminds us that life isn't about what we get, but what we give; not about the things in our lives, but how we choose to live. It's a powerful reminder to embrace every season with gratitude and grace. A reminder that there's a time to let go and a time to hold on, a time to press forward and a time to press pause, a time to seek solitude and a time to foster community.

Most of all, it's a reminder that we can all find beauty ~ even in the small, and seemingly ugly things.

Renee Edwards

Founder, Never Underestimate Simple, LLC.

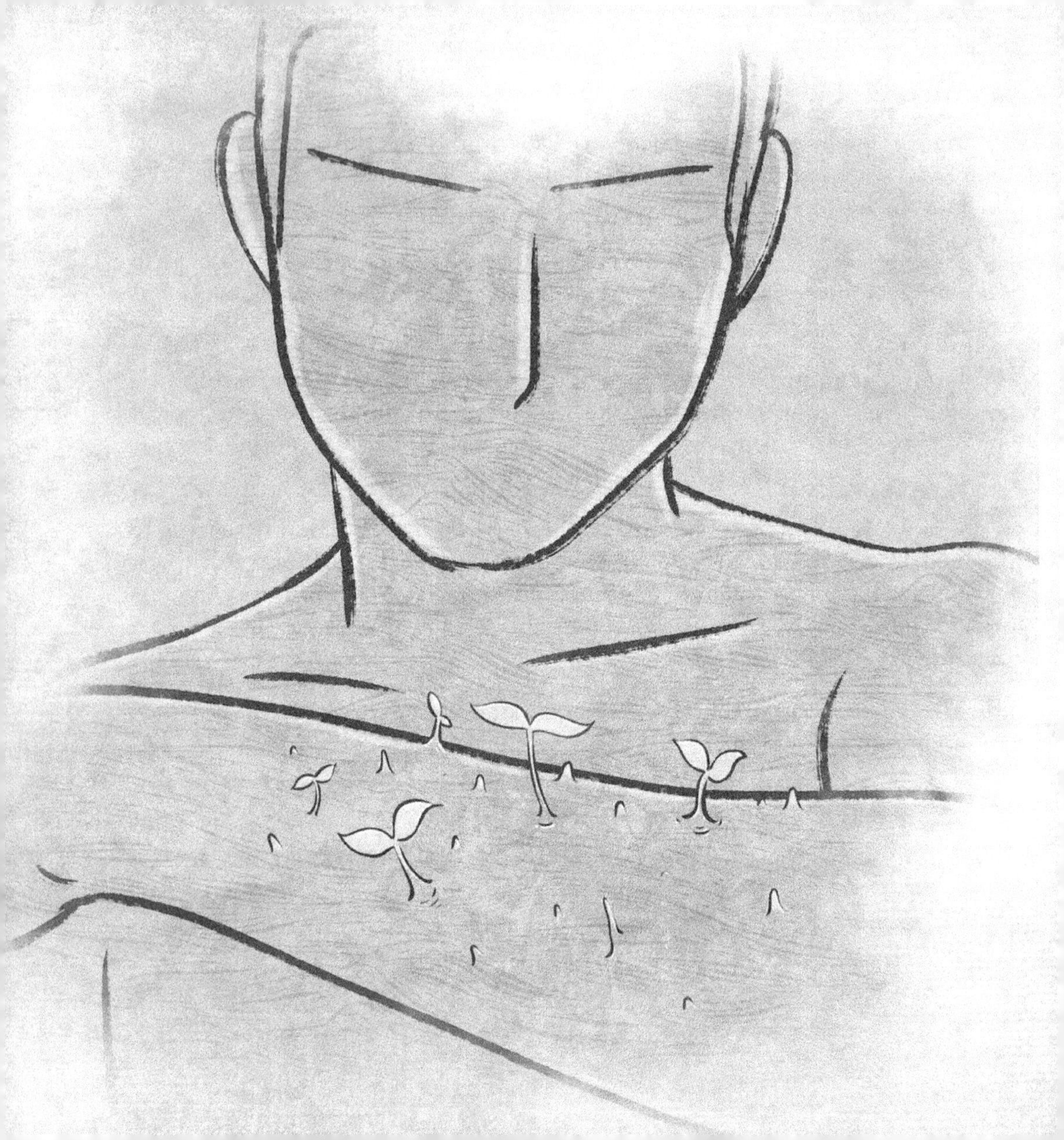

Today- creators gift

Your tomorrow seems uncertain, keep faith in your creator's plan
Your today is a blessing, break those shackles and jump as high as you can
It is here to make you dream, to conquer the rocks like a moving stream
Today is a day to take that extra step, to find a hurt and help them heal
The thing you do for others, will make you grow like a planted seed
Make the most of the present by filling a gap filling a need
It is a day to hug a loved one and tell them how you feel

It's your precious gift, it's your treasure don't let this slip away
Since you will shape your tomorrow from what you believe in today
Your words, the actions will help prepare the way
You will see tomorrow from what you say today

The clock is ticking, time is limited so work hard to get your pay
Coz you will reap tomorrow from what you sow today
The choice is yours, all you have this precious moment
In the sunlight of today
Where the dawn of tomorrow, meets the dusk of yesterday

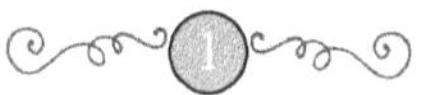

When the soul and ego met

On that fine morning my soul and ego met
Oh what a beautiful sight it was to be
It seemed the soul had too much to say about what this life is to be
With a small blink the soul started

Oh my ego, learn while still being a child
What this life is meant to be
To know it goes much beyond myself
It's just so much more than me

This life is about to learn to let go
While making a mistake be ready to bow
It is to overcome tragedy, survive the harder times
To face those moments filled with pain
And rather still be kind

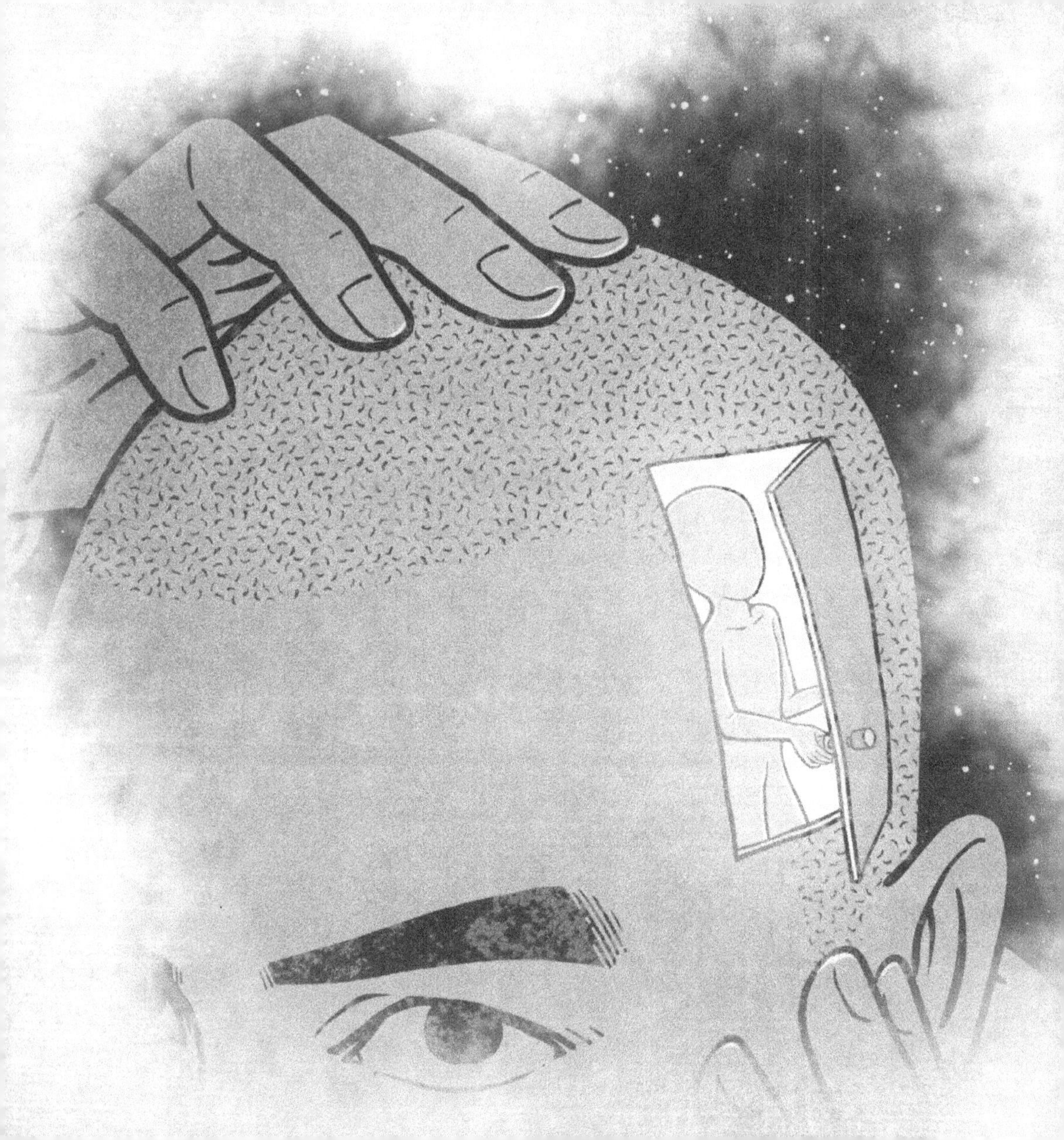

Don't just get lost in that mirror,
Rather try to understand the ones that no one cares to know
Make them feel of some value
When this world has let them go
Oh you ego, don't get lost in the me, rather focus on the we
Don't start to look at the prize rather enjoy this journey
This is what a life should be, this is what are all born for
To be of some worth and make a mark on planet earth

Let go

Hold on, Hold on are the only words I heard
They said hold on to cross that stream; hold on to live your dream
You're a beautiful bird, so hold on the tree to pass this thundering breeze
Look what the storm has done to the autumn leaves

Hold on, this big world is not one for you
It will twist you turn you make you blue
So hold on for long enough
Till the last tide, the last wind does not dance through

So I held on, I held on, they said that's how you'll know your strong
But not until I waited, I felt something wrong
All this while I thought holding on was bravery
But when the winds of change do blow and your inner strength shows
You realise that sometimes it's braver to just
Let go, Let go, Let go

Hi there, to my 15 year old shy young self
It's time to place your feet on the ground,
It's time to move on from the merry go round
As you get set to embark on this beautiful joy ride
Know the rules of the game; they will help you swim through the tide

The next few years will pass, in the blink of an eye
The good, the bag and the ugly all such times will fly by
The people you love will have come and gone
This world will never stop; you will have to carry on

As you trudge along, your life will be anything but easy
At every juncture struggles will be there
You'll learn to fill it with moments that matter, fill it with care
Stand on your own and find your way

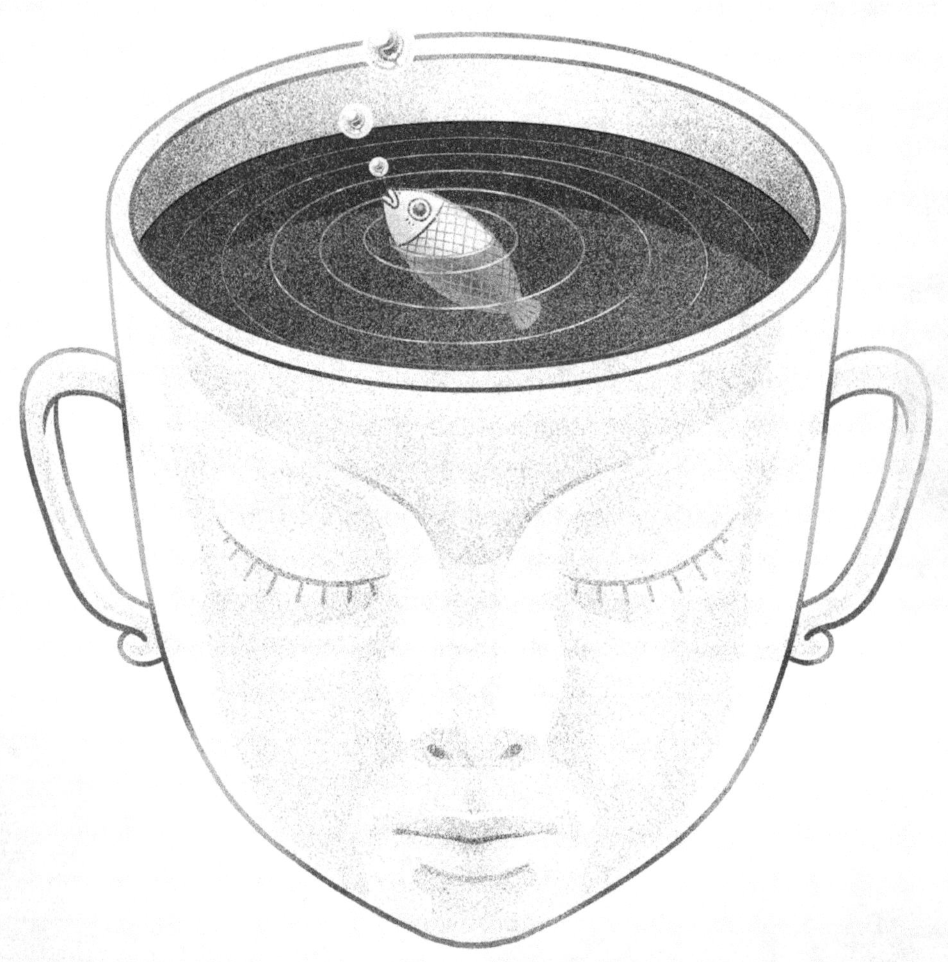

There will be nights filled with tears

But then, you will have the dawn of new days

The worries, the fears that plague you, will fade away

But how much you reach out to others in need

Will become your true measure to succeed

All that you share from your pure heart, is what will set you apart

So walk through the road, in times of adversity be brave

And remember life will never be about what you got, it will be all what you gave

Say thank you

Say thank you because your faith is so strong
It will help you cross that bridge from dusk to dawn
Say thank you beacause in the eye of the storm with the thunder so loud
Your creator has put a rainbow in the cloud

Say thank you because it'll help to transform your situation
It will help to alter your vibration
Say Thank you it will make you positive from the negative
It will teach you the art to always give

Say thank you beacause it will make your enough into more
It will be the key to open the happiness door
Say thank you to all those passengers on board
Because it's by saying thank you, you realise that this life is nothing
but a gift of the Lord

Still I'll rise

The dark clouds might enter the room with a thunder so loud
The sea might be rough with the tide so high
But like the sun, still I'll rise

The climb might look steep, the wild storm might make me blind
But like a wounded tiger, still I'll rise
You might knock me down, you might push me to drown
I'll take it all in my strive, with my hopes high still I'll rise
You may cut me down with your deceit, with your lies
You might look me down with your eyes
But still like the dust, I'll be up, I'll rise

Like an injured athlete, you must rise after every fall
Jump up and climb above all your walls
Coz you'll be a champ, if you look at every fall in the eye
And say I'll get up, still I'll rise

I see my girls in the mirror

Running around rugged streets, enjoying life even if it has to be bare feet
These angels enter this world without a silver spoon
Still make the most of every moment from night to noon
In a world full of deceit and lies
They remains happy with innocent filled eyes

They remain oblivious to the world and its changing trends
All they care about is to dance and maybe have a laugh with friends
I see my girls in the mirror,
They have their own burdens, face their own hardships and tests
Still they have a heart which is richer than the rest

Amidst all obstacles they teach me qualities of being patient and mild
These girls are special coz each of them are God's own child
I see my girls in the mirror
They've taught me to smile in a troubled time
They've taught me to live life even if it has to be under a cloudy sky

My furry friend!

With those beautiful black spots and a wagging tail
Cuddled in my arms, you entered my world, tiny and frail
Your presence made my every tear into one big smile
Holding you and walking was worth every mile

From morning to night, I could not do without you my precious furry friend
You were filled with mischief but faithful till the end
You looked at me with those eyes filled with love
Touching you always felt as soft as dove

Oh my friend, I loved you from the bottom of my heart
Wherever you go, these distances can never draw us apart
In my life you have left behind a beautiful trail
I will be here standing for you, until we don't meet again

The feeling that we call: Home

The road to those eyes of love and warm hugs beckons me
It's the road to all that's best, a road to my safety nest
The path where all is fine and fair and I see children run
For love and joy are waiting for me there, as soon as I am done

There is no reward or fame that I can compare with this
There is just the feeling of being loved a feeling of bliss
Amongst all the pleasures and palaces, I may roam
Being ever so humble I can say there's not a place like home

A place where I find the shining eyes that only see, the good I've tried to do
They think of me what I'd like to be; they know that I am true.
And whether I have lost my fight or whether I have won,
I find a faith that I've been right, no matter what I have done

This too shall pass

Today be grateful for life and its simple pleasures,
look at your silver lining it'll be your biggest treasure
Today feel happy for that never ending smile,
call a loved one to tell them you'll be there till the last mile
Today feel blessed for your friends,
tell them you'll be their shadow when the road bends
Today tell yourself you will wipe that tear,
you will walk ahead with courage and face every fear

Today look to count on all your blessings,
be thankful to life and all its teachings
Today live with the hope that'll you'll cross the bridge,
however treacherous be the ridge
Today fight your pains and move like a go getter
Be patient and you'll see life changing for the better

Today tell yourself it's just that matter of time,
your sun will come out and shine bright
Things will work out and it's going to be just alright
The clouds will move away, your worries will not last
Coz today tell yourself to remember that 'This too shall pass'"!

People need people

People need people, friends need friends
We all need someone to fall back on, someone on whom we can depend
We don't need too much of that bookish knowledge, just the feeling of being
understood
This feeling is enough to make our everyday feel good

People need people, just to express and share
To always be our strengths and make us aware
To have a laugh with and at times give a lending ear
To be able to hold us and wipe that tear

People need people, we don't need too much of acclaim or fame
We just need someone who can keep us in their prayers
That someone who can just look back and say Yes I care

To a loved one!

When I see you, there are many things the heart wants to say
In the mixed of many emotions, it's the eyes that give my words a way
I'll be there with you when you fall, but I'll also be the first to help you stand tall
I'll let you walk in the storm, but then I'll also cover you as a tree
I'll always be there behind you, yes you can always count on me

I'll be there with you when you first fail,
But I'll also be there to give that push for you to sail
I'll be there with you when you succeed,
But I'll also be there with you to always ground your feet

I'll always be there for you in every juncture of your life,
But I'll also be there with you when times are not right
Our bond is special, where not much is said
It is an emotion which is just heart felt!

Believe

In this world you try to be many things
But the people around tell you can't be anything
When those clouds loom high, remember you will be the light in the dark
In the night sky you will shine as the brightest star

In a room of many, you will be one of a kind
You have a bright soul which can never be confined
When the roads get rocky, like a flower you will blossom
You will show that you have it in you from winter to autumn
Believe in yourself that you can reach
Even when those around say the goal is bleak
Believe in yourself that you can scale every peak
Even when people say it's hard to achieve
People will always put you down
But I know you will come out stronger to never drown

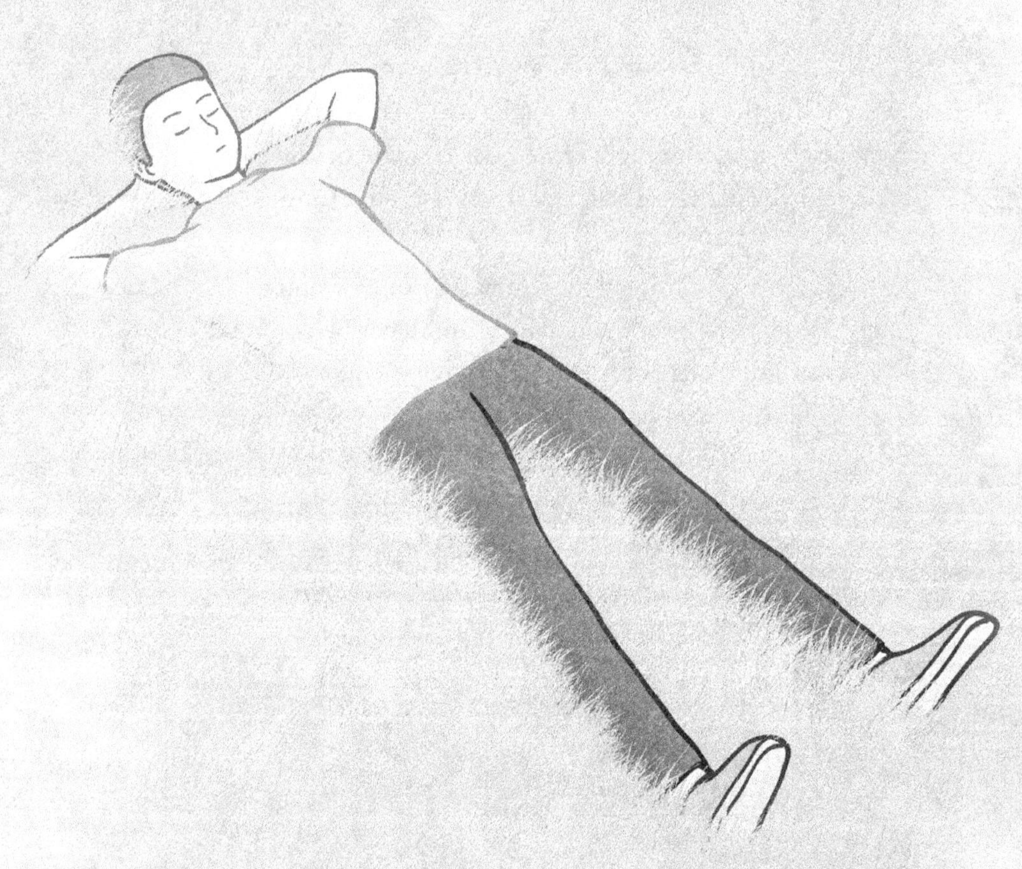

Just like the sun fights its way through the clouds
I know you will chart your way in the crowd
Just believe in yourself to find the best that is you
I know you will prevail and steer a course that is true

An evening on the bike!

I went for an evening bike ride

Crossing the dog stares and the by lanes, I went on to the country side

While biking it struck me that this ride is nothing but a journey of life

While biking you find some who stop you and some who give you side

It's the same in life, you find the good bad ugly, you just take them in your stride

While biking, I found parts where I sailed through but I did have my share of the climb

Just like the way our life is a mix of some happy and some testing times

While biking, I had to go on moving to keep my balance

Just like in life, you need to be on the move to overcome every challenge

While biking, it was the small things that drew my attention, from bells ringing to the sun setting

Just like in life, how it's the smaller things that make life worth living

This beautiful bike ride helped me discover some treasures of life

It made me a bit more aware a bit more wise!

Ice Cream

When life happens

While driving the car, I saw a boy selling ice creams
I waved at him and gave him my best smile
He stared back at me with that shine n sparkle in his eyes
It's in moments like these when the beauty of this life unravels
It's in moments like these when life happens

The other day I felt insecure so I asked a friend how to feel tall
He smiled, held my hand and said it's simple just bow down, that's all
In his words of wisdom, I felt the beauty of life unravel
It's moments like these when life happens

Every evening I would see a bird come on this mango tree
After a few evenings I see this bird had made a nest on the tree
On a stormy evening, I could see that same bird protect its baby
I again could see the beauty of life unravel
I could see life happen

All this while I would keep yearning for life's true pleasures
Little did I know that it lay in these small treasures
Live with an open heart to feel life's beauties unravel
Keep that love and you'll see life happen

Find your friendship

Over the years one starts to realise in any relation be it a mother daughter, or a husband wife relation, friendship should be the base of any and every relationship.

The moment you find friendship in your relationships it becomes that of trust, fun, transparency and a relationship where you can share with an open heart!!! Try and find friendship in your relationships today and you'll start to find beauty in them!

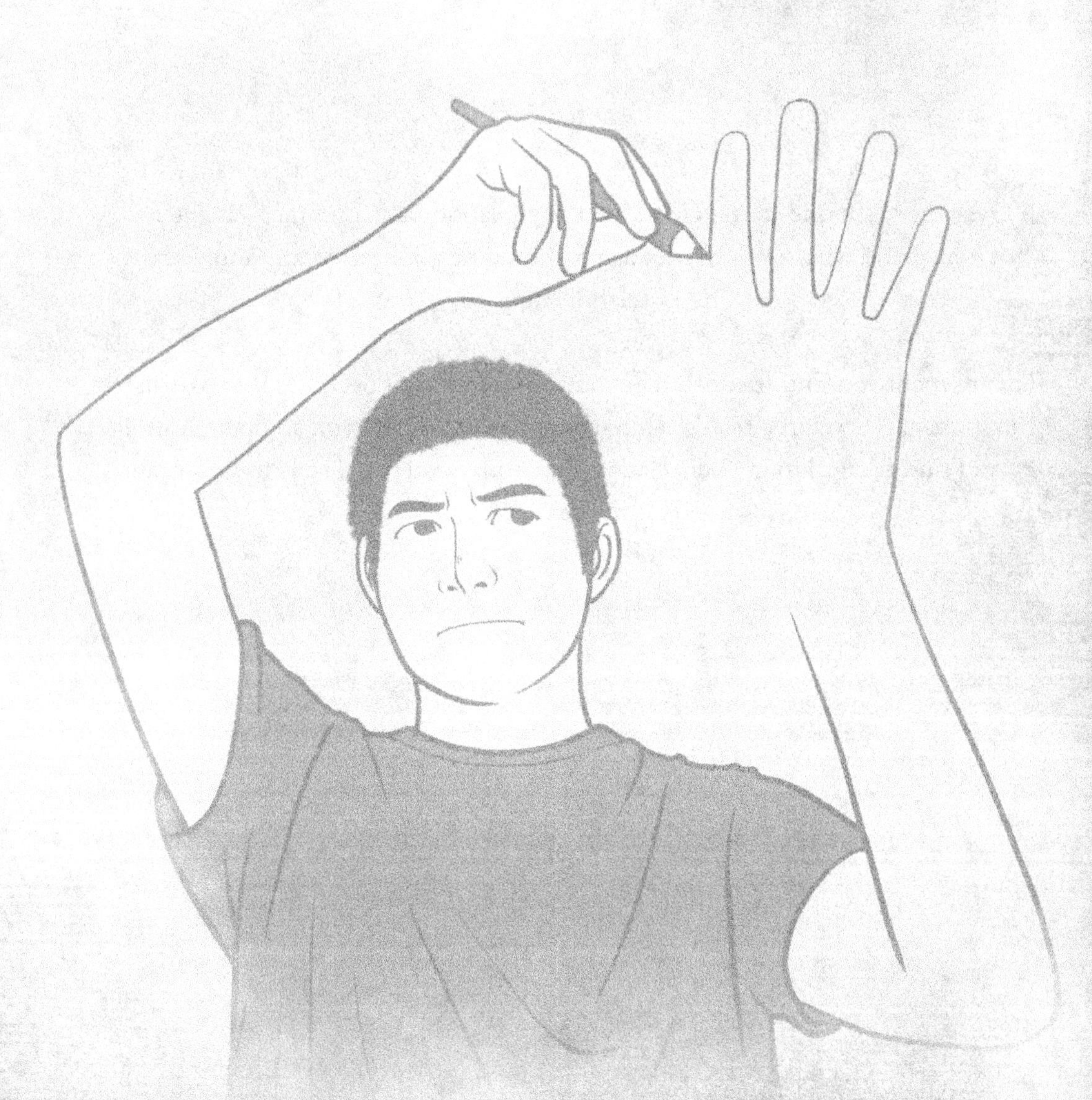

Be yourself

What a world it can be
Imagine if you and I can just walk free
With your hair down, walking without looking at the frowns
Listening to a bit of your heart a bit of your mind,
telling yourself you are a rare find

What a world it can be
If not the body but it's the soul that you and I can see
Living and loving this life with a free spirit
Making a difference in this world by doing your own bit

Let's make this a world that you and I want to see
By breaking those shackles and doing what you believe
This world will love you for who you are
Be yourself, be that original shining star!!!

Kindness

As you move on in your path of life
You'll find those crooked roads, you'll see a rainy day
But always carry that kindness in your heart
It'll pave your way, it might make someone's day

A simple smile can change the course of someone's week
These small gestures bring us all the happiness that we really seek

A gentle touch reminds us that humanity still reigns
To pet a lonely dog or cat shows that love will never wane
There will be a million obstacles on any given day
But rise above the hate and fear and live the kindness way
Trust me you would have made this world a much better place

I will be the person who stands with you in every journey you embark
I'll also be the person who is your moonlight while it's dark
I'll be the person who is loyal to you till the end
I'll also be the person who makes the mistake and then tries to amend

I'll be the person who is your constant source of hope
I'll aspire to be that person with whom you can share your heart and soul
I'll be with you so you learn to show love to both friends and foes
So you can spread your light wherever you go

I'll be with you so you learn what this life is meant to be
It's so much more than just you and me
I'll be with you so you value what this life is for
It's a gift given by God and it's for us to make it so much more
I'll be with you so you learn at the end life will never be about what take , it'll
always be about what you gave

Straight from My Heart

Ignite the Spark

Paintings and Poems by
Vedika Khaitan

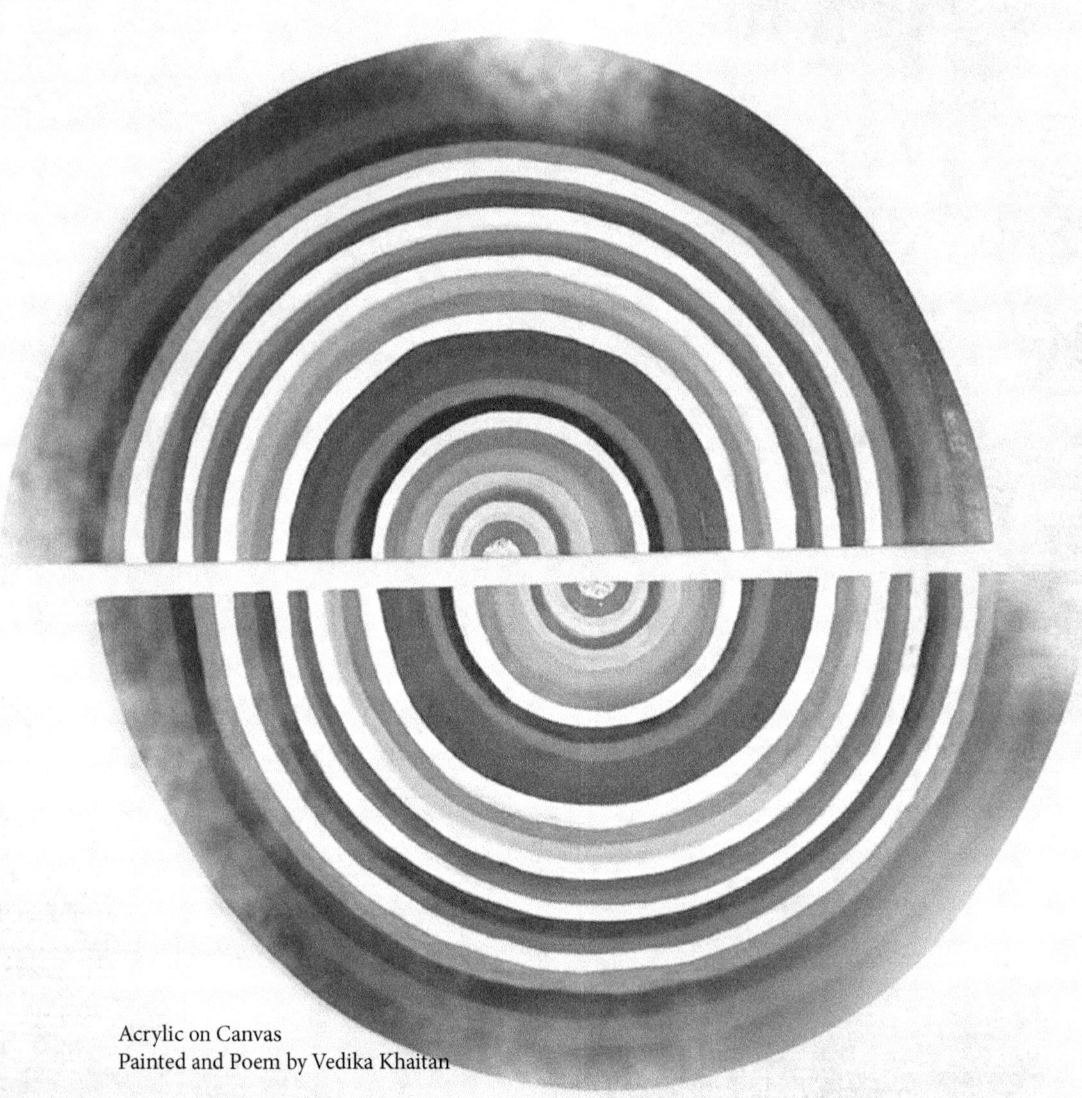

Acrylic on Canvas
Painted and Poem by Vedika Khaitan

Phase

Centred at the radiant soul,
We advance through every phase of life.

Each chapter brings something new,
Something dim, Something bright;

Adding each layer of experience to our being;
Compelled to make choices Some limiting, Some freeing;

Looking back at the past
What baggage to leave behind &
What memories to carry forward?

In the Present moment
What occurrences to accept &
What aspects to change?

For the future

What visions to build &
What challenges to overcome?

We ride the waves - Some strong, Some weak;
It is not the final destination that we seek,

Embracing the journey from start to end;
Or shall we say the Beginning Again.

Acrylic on Canvas
Painted and Poem by Vedika Khaitan

Mirror mirror on the wall

You reflect what we are - big or small;

The thoughts we give out to the world,
Bounce right back like a swirl;

For in between black and white
Exists every gray - dark or light;
Some days dull, Some days bright;
Deepest trenches to the highest height.

Mirror Mirror on the wall,
You reflect our hearts innermost call;

What we see in the person in front,
Is a reflection of our inner heed & hunt;
Everything we may open or hide,
All there is in or out of sight;

A little bit of me, A little bit of you,
Ingredients to the perfect stew;

Mirror Mirror on the Wall
You reflect what we are,
You show it all.